RAND

Conference Proceedings

Demography and Security

Proceedings of a Workshop
Paris, France
November 2000

Laurent Murawiec and David Adamson, editors

Supported by the
William and Flora Hewlett Foundation
David and Lucile Packard Foundation
Rockefeller Foundation

POPULATION MATTERS
A RAND Program of Policy-Relevant Research Communication

The research described in this report was supported by the William and Flora Hewlett Foundation, the David and Lucile Packard Foundation, and the Rockefeller Foundation.

ISBN: 0-8330-3065-5

RAND is a nonprofit institution that helps improve policy and decisionmaking through research and analysis. RAND® is a registered trademark. RAND's publications do not necessarily reflect the opinions or policies of its research sponsors.

Published 2001 by RAND
1700 Main Street, P.O. Box 2138, Santa Monica, CA 90407-2138
1200 South Hayes Street, Arlington, VA 22202-5050
201 North Craig Street, Suite 102, Pittsburgh, PA 15213-1516
RAND URL: http://www.rand.org/
To order RAND documents or to obtain additional information, contact Distribution Services: Telephone: (310) 451-7002; Fax: (310) 451-6915; Email: order@rand.org

Preface

In November 2000, a group of population scholars, security analysts, and interested observers gathered in Paris, France, to discuss demographic trends and their implications for international security. This document summarizes these discussions.

The conference was sponsored jointly by RAND's *Population Matters* project, the Institut national d'études démographiques (INED), the Société de Stratégie, RAND's Center for Middle East Public Policy, and RAND Europe.

The primary focus of *Population Matters* is synthesizing and communicating the findings and implications of existing research in ways that policy analysts and others will find accessible. The *Population Matters* project is funded by grants from the William and Flora Hewlett Foundation, the David and Lucile Packard Foundation, and the Rockefeller Foundation. This document should be of interest to anyone concerned with demographic trends and issues and their security implications. For further information on the *Population Matters* project, contact

> Julie DaVanzo, Director, *Population Matters*
> RAND
> 1700 Main St.
> P.O. Box 2138
> Santa Monica, CA 90407-2138
> Julie_DaVanzo@rand.org

Or visit the project's Web site at http://www.rand.org/labor/popmatters

Contents

Introduction

Laurent Murawiec and David Adamson, **RAND**

Background

Institutions that shape public policies on health care, insurance, education, and economics have long been producers and consumers of demographic information. Indeed, demography as a science can trace one of its major roots in actuarial calculation by British insurance companies that needed to evaluate the price and cost of annuities, and Swiss financiers who used Genevan maidens with exceptional longevity to purchase said annuities.

By contrast, the wealth of empirical observation, analysis, and prediction generated by demographers has not found its proper place in the thinking of some of its most important potential consumers: the foreign affairs, strategic, and defense communities. These areas, which could usefully integrate demographic consideration into their policy planning, have only sporadically paid attention. Demographic shifts are a cause, an effect, and a forerunner of geopolitical shocks and transformations. Their study should be one of the first steps in any form of strategic estimate. It may be that the academic and professional tracks of the demographic community and the strategic and defense communities do not naturally intersect. Providing venues for such intersections is therefore important. Once both communities are drawn into the same room and are given a chance to hear each other, however, the complementarity and mutual usefulness of their respective work promptly becomes visible. This is certainly what happened at the "Demography and National Security" workshop held in Paris in November 2000 at the initiative of RAND's *Population Matters* project.

The workshop brought together senior representatives from the French Ministry of Defense; American, French, and other European demographers; economists; and experts in geopolitics whose different angles of vision created something of a stereoscopic view of the subject at hand: the impact of demographic phenomena on the geostrategic evolution of the world.

Enlightening differences were obvious, both between demographers and national-security experts, but also between American and French participants. Different objects of concern and of research appeared, and contrasting views of phenomena. Immigration, for instance, was seen in an altogether different light on the two sides of the Atlantic, as were its social, cultural, and political impacts. Population-based threat analysis tends to enter the field of vision of Americans far more than that of Europeans. Americans tend to use demography as a forecasting tool for foreign policy, while Europeans are more likely to focus on domestic affairs.

Summary

The opening presentation, by RAND's Brian Nichiporuk, set forth a general framework for understanding the security relevance of particular demographic trends. Negligible population growth in the industrial nations implies an increased reliance on technological solutions to defense problems; by contrast, rapid population growth in developing countries suggests that human capital will continue to undergird national power in those countries; increased urbanization throughout the world makes urban conflict more likely; and ever-larger flows of migrants create potentially destabilizing forces in many regions of the world.

The presentations that followed each developed some aspect of this opening framework, either by focusing on particular regions of the world, providing historical background for understanding current trends, or examining the security implications of specific demographic factors such as immigrant flows, urbanization, and ethnic composition.

Two presentations examined demographic trends and their security implications in specific geographic areas: Russia and the greater Middle East.

Julie DaVanzo of RAND examined the grim demographic situation in Russia. Low fertility and high mortality from preventable causes have resulted in negative population growth in Russia. Though some opponents of post-Communist reform have blamed economic and social change for these conditions, long-term trends suggest that high alcohol consumption and the failing health care system are key culprits. Economic turmoil has played a part, but the dire trends in Russia have been building for decades. The main security concern for Russia is the declining size of the military-age population. Coupled with economic problems that are likely to severely limit force modernization, population decline is weakening the Russian military.

Brian Nichiporuk of RAND, in his second presentation, explored the demographic roots of conflict in the Greater Middle East, where urbanization and a burgeoning youth population are contributing to resource shortages, unemployment, and unrest.

Two presentations examined the historical dimensions of current demographic trends and discussed their implications.

Jean-Claude Chesnais of INED focused on the historic parallelism of demographic evolution and the geopolitics of power. He argued that population size and composition are still an important consideration in national power and security planning. The potentially disruptive presence of Islamic immigrants and other diasporas is a security issue Western Europe has yet to fully confront.

Laurent Murawiec of RAND challenged the assumption that population size and composition are still relevant to national power. He noted that the relationship between numbers and age structure on the one hand, and the production of wealth and war-fighting on the other hand, has undoubtedly changed with the kind of post-transition demographic regime specific to the information age.

Four presentations examined the implications of specific population factors: falling fertility, immigration flows, urbanization, and shifting ethnic composition.

Philippe Bourcier de Carbon of INED discussed low fertility and negative population growth in the world's industrial nations and showed how these have defied demographic models prevalent in the postwar decades, with serious consequences for Western nations.

Stephan DeSpiegeleire of RAND Europe offered a contrarian view of international migration's impact. Looking at case studies of "sending" nations, he argued that international migration can actually have a stabilizing effect by creating a "safety valve" to defuse problems tied to overpopulation in "sending" countries and by improving relations between the sending and destination countries.

General Eric de la Maisonneuve of the Société de Stratégie examined the implications of growing urbanization. The epoch-making shift of warfare from its traditional venue—the countryside—to urban settings is having a revolutionary impact on modern ways of war.

Noël Bonneuil of INED focused on theories of causation of ethnic conflicts. He concluded that policies to contain ethnic conflict should focus more clearly on economic and social mobility.

The animated debate that followed proved to all participants that they had only begun to scratch the surface. This was virtually a mandate for further such exercises.

SUMMARIES OF
CONFERENCE PAPERS

A Framework for Examining the Relationship Between Demographic Factors and Security Issues[1]

Brian Nichiporuk, **RAND**

This presentation offered a general framework for considering the relationship between demographic factors and security issues. It examined (1) global demographic trends, (2) the security implications of these, and (3) the policy implications for the United States and other Western nations.

Global Demographic Trends

Fertility trends in the industrialized world and those in the less industrialized countries have begun to diverge sharply in recent years. The developed nations are characterized by chronic low fertility. The low rates in European nations such as Spain, Italy, and France—as well as those in some Asian nations, notably Japan—seem to have no parallels in history. Pronatalist policies have been unsuccessful in increasing fertility rates significantly. The developing world is bifurcating into two types of countries—those lowering their fertility rates (for example, Brazil and Indonesia) and those with continuing high fertility rates, which are mostly in sub-Saharan Africa, the Middle East, and Central America.

As a result, the weight of global population is shifting away from the developed world toward the developing world. The top four most populous nations (China, India, the United States, and Indonesia) will remain the same over the next 20 years, but the bottom six in the top ten will change significantly. Japan and Russia may disappear from that list, while Nigeria, Pakistan, and Bangladesh will likely move up; perhaps Ethiopia will move up as well. In addition, there will still be robust population growth in the developing world overall. Demographic growth and pressures will be greatest between now and 2025, when growth is likely to abate.

A second important trend is urbanization. Over half of the world's population now lives in urban areas, and urban concentrations in many nations are becoming disproportionately large. Projections suggest that more than 20 megacities (cities of 10 million or larger) will exist by 2015.

A third trend is also cause for concern: The number of refugees (moving across borders) continues to be problem, amounting to over 14.4 million in 1995, the latest year for which information is available.

---

[1] This presentation is based on Brian Nichiporuk, *The Security Dynamics of Demographic Factors* (RAND MR-1088, 2000).

Security Implications

These trends suggest three potential changes in the global security environment.

(1) Changes in the nature of conflict. There is likely to be an increased prevalence of urban conflict (also discussed in the paper by de la Maissoneuve, below). Urban conflict tends to be attractive to insurgents and guerrilla forces, in part because it can equalize conflict between technologically sophisticated and less sophisticated armed forces.

Ethnic diasporas are also likely to see their influence increase. Information technology, such as the Internet, is creating more opportunities for emigrant populations to influence conflict in home countries very quickly. The Tamil diaspora and Kosovar Albanians provide examples of this.

In addition, water is likely to become increasingly important as a strategic tool in some areas of the world, especially where water systems are overburdened.

(2) Changes in sources of national power. Differential fertility rates also have implications for sources of military power in low- and high-fertility states. Low-fertility states will be increasingly forced to substitute technology for manpower. By contrast, militaries of high-fertility states will build a two-tiered force structure, with a smaller elite force and larger but less-skilled and less well-equipped force.

(3) Changes in sources of conflict. It does not appear that demographic forces will necessarily change the conventional balances of power. Changes in population growth rates are less of a factor in shifting this balance than they were 40 or 50 years ago. Instead, a major new demographic factor that will influence conflict is refugee flows (for example, the flow of Kosovars into Macedonia).

In addition, relatively young populations—"youth bulges" in the population pyramid—increase the tendency toward violence. This risk is present in many Middle Eastern nations, such as Egypt and Libya. Historically, it was an important factor in the Algerian civil war.

Differential growth rates in neighboring culture groups or populations can also lay the groundwork for ethnic conflict. In Bosnia, for example, fears of Muslim growth in control, fueled by collapse of the Yugoslav state apparatus, fueled ethnic strife (see the paper by Bonneuil for further discussion of ethnic conflict).

Implications for United States and Western Nations

There are three principal security-related steps the United States and its Western allies can take to respond to these trends:

1. Increase information collection and analysis of indicators of impending conflict, especially on warning signs related to refugee flows.

2. Conduct more analysis on the security effects of nonmilitary foreign aid, such as development funding. Have these had stabilizing effects and strengthened moderate regimes? If so, how are these effects to be measured?

3. Increase planning for urban warfare. In the near term, training is the most important issue. Over the long-term, new capabilities, such as unmanned aerial vehicles, will be vital to help militaries adapt successfully to the urban setting.

Dire Demographics: Population Trends in Russia[2]

Julie DaVanzo, **RAND**

This presentation discussed Russia's demographic situation, particularly recent population loss; reviewed some explanations for these trends and their plausibility; and explored broad policy implications of the current situation. Recent demographic trends in Russia have caused widespread concern among Russian policymakers and the general public. Three trends are causing the greatest concern: low fertility and consequent population loss; historically high abortion rates; and falling life expectancy and increased mortality.

Population Loss and Low Fertility

The dissolution of the Soviet Union caused Russia's global population status to change: Once part of the third most populous nation in the world (the USSR), Russia was only the 6th most populous in 2000. By 2010, Russia's population is projected to decline from 145 million to 142 million, which will place it 9th among the world's nations. Fertility rates in Russia declined throughout the 20th century. From 7 children per woman in 1900, the total fertility rate fell to 1.17 in 1999. Though sharp, these declines are not sharply distinct from those in other industrialized nations, many of which (including France, Spain, Italy, and Japan) are experiencing birth rates below replacement level (2.1 children per woman). Nonetheless, Russia's current fertility rate places it among the lowest in the world.

High Abortion Rates

Only Cuba, Romania, and Vietnam—all countries that also have a Communist history—have higher rates of abortion than Russia. About 7 in 10 pregnancies in Russia end in abortion; by comparison, in the United States, less than 3 in 10 do. High rates of abortion in Russia lead to health problems: Two in three Russian women who have abortions suffer health complications that require medical care or hospitalization, placing a burden on an already weak health care system. Abortion rates have dropped since contraception became more widely available after the fall of communism, but continue to pose public health concerns.

---

[2] For further information, see Julie DaVanzo and Clifford Grammich, *Dire Demographics: Population Trends in the Russian Federation* (forthcoming, RAND MR-1273, 2001).

Falling Life Expectancy and Increasing Mortality

The most worrisome trend is the downturn in life expectancy and the increase in rates of mortality. The health and mortality of a population can be summarized by life expectancy at birth—the number of years a child born in a particular year can be expected to live if at each age he or she experiences the age-specific death rates of that year. Since 1970, life expectancy for Russian women, once nearly equivalent to that for U.S. women, has stagnated or declined slightly. Today, life expectancy for Russian women is about 8 years lower than that for U.S. women. The situation is even worse for men. In the early 1990s, life expectancy for Russian men declined sharply. Today, life expectancy for Russian men is 14 years lower than that for U.S. men. Male life expectancy in Russia is now lower than that for Mexico, Indonesia, the Philippines, Egypt, and Iraq. Russian males born today can expect to live an average of about 60 years. Russian females have a life expectancy of about 72 years. This difference of 12 years in life expectancy is the largest differential by sex in the world.

What accounts for these life expectancy and mortality trends? Several explanations have been proposed for these alarming mortality trends:

- *Environmental degradation?*

No. Environmental problems cannot explain mortality variations, why mortality rates are higher for men than for women, or why they rose most for people of working age.

- *Varying levels of alcohol consumption?*

Yes. Mortality trends in the 1980s and 1990s are directly related to trends and patterns of alcohol consumption

- *Deterioration of the health care system?*

Yes, in the long term; but health care is less important for short-term changes.

- *Consequences of economic changes?*

Yes, somewhat. The contraction of the Russian economy during the 1990s (when GDP per capita fell by 40 percent), poverty, and the stress caused by the transformation do seem to help explain the decrease and variations in life expectancy in the 1990s.

Addressing Health and Population Concerns

There are several measures that can be undertaken now to address population and health issues in Russia.

- Increased access to contraceptives can help Russia continue to cut its abortion rates and curb maternal health problems and deaths attributable to illegal abortions.

- Russia can strengthen and expand public health education programs, including those to reduce tobacco and alcohol consumption.

- The health care system is outdated and needs to be improved.

- Most likely, addressing Russia's demographic problems will require broad solutions. Pronatalist policies have had little effect. An antialcohol campaign during Gorbachev's tenure was effective but unpopular. Immigration is unlikely to offset population decline and is politically sensitive.

Many of Russia's demographic problems or their consequences can be addressed, but these require stability and resources, both on the part of the government and individuals. The deepest demographic problems will likely be solved only by long-term economic stability and resulting improvements in public finance. Several former communist states of eastern Europe that faced similar problems brought their mortality rates under control once they achieved macroeconomic stability, particularly sustained, noninflationary growth.

Security Implications

The steady decline in the number of births in Russia since 1987 means that the number of Russians of military age will soon be shrinking. This occurrence may raise concerns for the international community. Despite current plans to cut personnel to boost military spending per member, it is unclear to what extent Russia will be able to modernize its military. Its weak economy may prevent Russia from expending much capital on new military technology, and its peculiar position in the international community may prevent it from allying with wealthier nations for joint development of new military hardware and technology. At the same time, Russia may have trouble defending its huge land mass, as well as its more than 12,000 miles (20,000 km) of borders if military forces are reduced. Such pressures may force Russia to rely on weapons of mass destruction, including nuclear weapons, for its security.

Security Implications of Demographic Factors in the Middle East

Brian Nichiporuk, **RAND**

Population Trends in the Middle East

Population trends in the Middle East—defined broadly to include the area from the Persian Gulf to Turkey and Egypt—have several important implications for the region's security.

1. Population growth and fertility rates remain robust in most Middle East nations. Only Turkey and Israel have fertility rates below 3.0 children per woman.

2. The populations of most Middle East states are relatively young, and many states host sizable ethnic minority groups.

3. The area's population is becoming increasingly urbanized.

4. Population flows within the region have created mixed settlement regions, where there are large ethnic diasporas and increasing transborder mobility.

5. Population pressures in the region confront many states with shortages of fresh water.

6. The region is characterized by extensive guest worker flows from labor-exporting countries like Egypt to labor-importing countries like Saudi Arabia.

External factors are also creating a volatile backdrop. Notably, these include fluctuations in oil prices and the many leadership transitions in the area, including those in Jordan, Iran, Morocco, and Bahrain.

Security Implications

What are the main security implications of these trends? Three are most prominent:

First, the nature of conflict may be affected. Growing urbanization increases the likelihood that conflicts will be either urban-centered or have an important urban component. In addition, during crises, water has the potential to become a weapon in conflicts between neighboring states.

Second, the sources of nations' military power could be affected. Traditionally, populous states with high birth rates and large youth populations have drawn on their plentiful supply of young manpower to populate large, manpower-intensive armies. However, it is becoming more difficult to translate burgeoning populations into a source of effective military power. There are three reasons for this:

- Technologies associated with the information revolution in military affairs technology (information processing, sensors, targeting tools) are increasingly available and significant.

- The open desert terrain found in much of the Middle East favors technology-intensive forces over traditional conventional forces.

- Technology-intensive forces require good logistics, training, and integration for effectiveness.

As a result, conventional Middle East balances of power are becoming less sensitive to differential population size/growth. Furthermore, there are incentives to depend on weapons of mass destruction and a small number of elite conventional warfare divisions (e.g., Iraq's Republican Guards) for external conflicts.

Sources of conflict may also shift. Large youth populations and urbanization are contributing to higher levels of perceived relative deprivation in many Arab states. Some of these states are experiencing shortages of housing and land, underemployment, strained infrastructures, and pollution.

In this kind of environment, certain "triggering mechanisms" can be catalysts for spontaneous violence, including sudden price hikes for basic food stuffs, mass transit, and education. These events are often due to external variables (such as International Monetary Fund directives). For example, in 1988 food price increases triggered violence in Algeria; likewise, "bread riots" occurred in Jordan in 1996. The resulting unrest from such an event could lead to revolution or civil war, depending on the strength of strength of Islamist organizations, the level of political alienation among the "masses," and the rate of ongoing social change.

Friction in majority–minority relations may also emerge as a source of conflict, as in the case of the strife between Coptic Christians and Muslims in Egypt.

The Decolonization of Europe

Jean-Claude Chesnais, INED

Are numbers still an important issue when considering the relationship between population and national security? This paper examines this question by looking at historical trends. It combines two approaches: one historical, the other analytical.

Global Trends

The past few centuries witnessed a "Europeanization" of the globe, during the phase of population explosion. Now, as a result of conditions created by that experience, the world is experiencing a "de-Europeanization," linked to population stagnation, contrasting with the spread and magnitude of the population explosion occurring in the developing world. In 1950, Europe had 17 percent of the world's population; now it has only 12 percent. The best illustration of this "de-Europeanization" has been the progress of decolonization in places like India, the Soviet Empire, and the African empires. It is unclear how far this trend will go—the extent to which, for instance, Russia will break up into different ethnic nation-states. In many ways, decolonization was a political necessity because the "mother countries" lacked the resources and population to promote development of the increasingly populous colonies.

In the past, population growth and size played a major role in the geopolitics of power. Up until about 1940 it favored Europe and had for 500 years, during the phase in which Europe experienced very high growth. Up until World War II, Europe and the United States experienced high population growth, contrasting sharply with most of the colonies.

Take the United Kingdom, for example. How did such a small island gain dominion over so much of the world? It can be argued that high population growth in the 18th and 19th centuries provided a demographic surplus and thus fueled imperialist impulses. The aftermath: The U.K. "gave birth" to the United States, Canada, Australia, New Zealand, and South Africa. Likewise, the Irish diaspora was fueled by high birth rates and high population growth in Ireland. Russia is also an interesting case. In 1900, the United States and Russia had the highest fertility rates in the world. In the century that followed, both nations pursued imperialist expansion fueled by explosion of earlier high population growth. Is it coincidence that the world was roughly divided between these two powers in the late 20th century?

France provides a contrary example. France was an imperial force for centuries and had expansionist ambitions and power that far outstripped her neighbors. France, though, has had low birth rates since the time of the French Revolution. During the 19th and 20th centuries, France was unable to fend off its more populous neighbor, Germany, which invaded France three times in 70 years. French colonialism was also peculiar: in contrast to the overflow colonialism of Great Britain, France did not populate its colonies with French natives. Algeria, for instance, was a Department of France, but never a major destination for French emigration.

The imperialist explosion led to the lesser populated half of the world becoming more populated. The Americas and Oceania, for example, went from a population of 22 million in the year 1700 to 900 million in 2000. Much of the growth was fueled by European emigration or colonization.

Another point illustrates the importance of demographics over a very long period of time. The United States had a population of 9 million in 1820, which grew to 280 million in 2000. The population of the United States could exceed the population of Europe (excluding Russia) if current trends continue. This suggests that American supremacy will extend for some time. The United States, however, is no longer primarily a European country. It has growing Asian, African, and Latin American populations.

Key Questions for the Future

The unfolding of this trend poses critical questions, especially for Europe, in the near future:

- What influence will population structure have? The aging population profiles already exert huge pressure on public expenditures.

- What are the implications of changing national ethnic composition? Can diasporas jeopardize feelings of national identity? The end of the prior order portends dramatic changes. Europe must address this question because foreign immigrants have brought Islam into Europe, raising the question of what will happen in the event of a global crisis involving Islam.

- Are U.N. statistics on country demographics still relevant? Current trends tend to involve groups of nations, like NAFTA and the European Union.

In conclusion, over the long term, it is still true that a nation's demographic profile is critical to its national power and national security, notwithstanding the military's ability to buy technological advantages.

An Amateur's Musings: Questions to Demographers

Laurent Murawiec, **RAND**

In traditional, rural-agrarian societies, the number of arms, the quantity of land, and the fertility of land linearly determine agricultural output, all things (weather, etc.) being equal. There is little technology ("artificial energy") available to multiply the results and transform productivity. When France's preeminent theorist of the absolute right of kings, Jean the Mercantilist Bodin, writes in the 16th century, "There is no wealth but in people" (*Il n'est richesse que d'homme*), a quantitative interpretation is apposite: The more subjects, the wealthier and mightier the king. Children, many of them, are both the principal productive force and the social security system. The extended family is society's building block, as Ferdinand Tönnies showed in his classic *Gesellschaft und Gemeinschaft* analysis of the transition from the agrarian to the industrial world.

In industrial societies, large populations translate into large numbers of producers and large numbers of consumers. The Industrial Revolution—if we understand by this a process that stretched over many centuries—boosted population growth and in return was powered by population growth, in virtuous cycle. The core system of economic life correlates the number of people employed to the technology they command and the mode of organization applied to produce: productivity per unit of capital and per unit of labor. In that context, the family tends to shrink in numbers and in intergenerational spread: It is not an extended family anymore (akin to clannish-tribal forms) but increasingly a nuclear family. From Bismarck onwards, social security systems are increasingly centralized, either through the state (Prussia, France) or privately.

In "postmodern" society, productivity comes to the fore as never before. In the Information Age, it is in cyberspace that the margins of progress and profit are highest. A knowledge-based economy does not require physical vigor and youth from its "workers," as opposed to agricultural and industrial modes of production. To be productive is to be creative. People who have not spent a lifetime in backbreaking work can have extended "postretirement" careers and need not stop being productive members of society at 60 or 65. "Retired" people may continue working; earning income from their labor, their accumulated experience is not lost. This is an economic engine. They also continue to consume: Not only are they receiving a pension, they also have lifetime savings and equity, which are individually owned and managed, and disposable income, as opposed to survival-income retirees of yore.

There is now, in other words, a historically unprecedented disconnect between numbers, ages, and economic growth. This disconnect is especially pronounced in those "developing" nations that are not developing, e.g., in Africa and large parts of the Middle East, where the abundance of the youth cohorts saturates existing infrastructures and capital available to generate jobs: population growth offsets economic growth, nullifying gains or creating a net loss. It is as though, *metaphorically* (I am not a sociobiologist), the human species was shifting from the biologists' strategy of maximizing numbers of offspring in hostile environments, to the strategy of optimizing investment in small numbers of offspring.

The disconnect has a major impact on defense and strategy—especially in the context of the "revolution in military affairs."[3] Can we go to war with fewer young men? Is the kind of war we plan to fight "competitive" from a demographic standpoint? Can we get rid of the "zero-casualty" mentality while preserving a rational kernel, to wit: that, in keeping with our post–demographic transition demographic regime, we invest far too much in each individual to want to venture their lives lightly? I would like demographers to tell me more about the demo-economics involved. This issue is not really clear to me.

---

[3] The "revolution in military affairs" is the "migration" to the military domain of the revolutions that have transformed the economy and civil society in the last quarter century: the digital revolution and the transformations in management and organization that resulted in decentralizing and modularizing the corporate sector.

Demographic Variations and Their Global Implications

Philippe Bourcier de Carbon, INED

This paper discusses current global demographic trends, especially in light of United Nations (U.N.) population projections, and examines some of their geopolitical implications.

U.N. population projections are based on obsolete fertility models. Premised on the "demographic transition" paradigm, these models assume that replacement level fertility (2.1 children per couple) is a norm at which industrializing countries' populations will stabilize. The models and their underlying assumptions triumphed at the 1984 Mexico City United Nations Population conference.

But reality has shown that U.N. projections have been flawed. In all countries where fertility has declined, the speed of this decline has been greater than projected, and nations in the later stages of the "transition" have seen fertility fall well below replacement level. Demographers have not created an alternative model for explaining such a fertility decline and the mechanisms that cause it.

What are the implications of these sharp declines in fertility? We may never hit the 8-billion world population level. Many European and East Asian nations are on the road to demographic decline. Somewhere between 10 and 40 percent of the world's nations are losing population. This decline has two characteristics: the concentration of population in large cities, and an inversion of the age pyramid in which the old outnumber the young.

As a result, societies in developed nations look different than ever before. The median age of EU voters is now over 50. The aging of populations in developed countries has led to a growth in the clout of older groups, to the detriment of their juniors in all aspects of life. In effect, we are witnessing a social, economic, and political eviction of young people.

This fact has substantial ramifications for policy directions. In developed countries, assets and power are becoming increasingly concentrated in the hands of senior citizens, who also increasingly absorb a large share of national productivity. This fact is likely to exacerbate the demographic "implosion," as increases in spending for the elderly exert further downward pressure on fertility decisions for the younger generation.

What is needed? National policies that encourage larger families and devote greater resources to those under 50. Contrary to received wisdom, pro-natalist policies carried out at national level could have worked. It has been argued that policies aimed at enlarging families have merely advanced the fertility schedules, as in Sweden. Analysis shows that it is not so. As European nations had to abide by the Maastricht criteria of fiscal balance, the costs of family policies were assessed to be too high, and the relevant budgets were slashed.

These facts show how ideology has distorted demographic analysis and, conversely, affected social policies. Europe is in an alarming situation, and action is urgently required.

Effects of Immigration on Domestic Stability in Sending Countries: Three Case Studies

Stephan DeSpiegeleire, **RAND**

Discourse about the domestic security implications of immigration has been distorted. Migration and migrant populations are almost invariably regarded as a destabilizing force and thus discussed as a security challenge to hosting countries. The bulk of the European literature on immigration is devoted to the negative consequences of emigrants on receiving countries. This view persists despite the scarcity of evidence that immigration is a significant cause of conflict. This perspective also ignores two important issues: the effect of immigration on sending countries, and the effect on relations between the sending and host countries.

Case Studies of Immigration's Effect on Sending Countries

What impact does immigration have on domestic stability? In order to address this question, I conducted three case studies, using examples of immigration to the United States from three different historic periods:

- Germany in the mid-19th century

- Japan in the early 20th century

- Mexico in the late 20th century

The study focused on the effects on the sending country. To attempt to capture this, the analysis used a complex variable for measuring "domestic stability."

The case studies suggested that international migration is actually more of a stabilizing than destabilizing force. There are two fundamental reasons for this: First, the sending of emigrants can act like a release valve, reducing pressures in the country of origin stemming from overpopulation and associated ills such as high unemployment, crime, or other forms of unrest. Indeed, *blocking* migration may actually cause more conflict than migration. For instance, the case study on Japan suggested that emigration in the early 19th century provided a kind of escape valve that enabled Japan to moderate the effects of rapid population growth and associated resource demands. When restrictionist U.S. policies stopped the flow of Japanese immigrants in the 1920s, the safety valve was blocked. This action helped to advance the agenda of pro-imperialist, expansionist interests within Japan, who argued that Japan was left with no choice but to expand by force into neighboring Asian territories. The regional consequences for East Asia are difficult to ignore: At the end of the 1920s, Japan began its expansionist moves into Manchuria. Likewise, the Mexican example suggested that the provinces that had sent the largest number of emigrants were the most stable.

Second, the presence of a large émigré community can actually strengthen ties between the destination country and the country of origin. The case study of Germany suggested that large numbers of German immigrants in the United States contributed to improved relations and increased mutual understanding between the United States and Germany in the 19th century.

War: From Countryside to Urban Settings

Eric de la Maisonneuve (Maj.-Gen., ret., French Army), **Chairman, Société de Stratégie**

War is a chameleon, as Clausewitz put it. It also has a way of penetrating every breach in human affairs. War has long ago exceeded the fragile limits once ascribed to it and is increasingly invading the proliferating urban territories of today's world. Urban battlefields are disquietingly unregulated, savage, and dangerous.

In Renaissance and Classical-Age Europe, war was regulated and ruled by strict principles. With the Westphalian Peace of 1648, war became the exclusive preserve of States. States waged war against each other by means of professional armies; soldiers maximized the rational use of resources in a well-defined theater of action—in most cases, the countryside. War took place in the country, in the "field." The military vocabulary bears witness to that: *campaign*, battle*field*, etc. At stake was the conquest of territory. The paradox of war in an urban setting is that the city's very functions are disorganized and destroyed by combat occurring in it. This is why it was traditionally avoided. Cities may have been destroyed by conquerors (Tamerlaine), but fighting was taking place elsewhere. War-fighting in cities always was costly, cumbersome, and dangerous.

During World War I, war burst free of its earlier limits: It became worldwide and mobilized all resources, spaces, and people. Cities were annexed to the territory of war: Verdun, Stalingrad, Leningrad. European and Japanese cities were devastated by artillery and strategic bombing. In the nuclear age, the cities became the principal target of the mutually assured destruction regime. The colonial wars also witnessed this shift of warfare from countryside to city. In "revolutionary wars," cities—e.g., Algiers, Hue—became paramount. Urban terrorism acquired a new importance. Western armies were trapped in the cities. Recent civil wars, or identity wars—in the Balkans, in the Middle East, in Africa—are largely urban: Beirut, Mogadishu, Grozny, Sarajevo, etc.

In its urban setting, hatred as a fundamental psychological motive becomes anew the driving force of war: the extermination of the other becomes the aim of war. Traditional armies are unable to cope with this kind of situation. A division-based Army is maladapted to this kind of conflict. Invisible and fluid ethnic frontiers do not compose well-defined fronts. The role of intelligence has to be transformed and maximized. Urban warfare–capable equipment (vehicles, weapon systems) has to be used. Training and organization must also be adapted.

Today, the choice is this: Either we feel morally obligated and geopolitically compelled to involve ourselves in such conflicts, in which case we urgently must adapt our forces to the requirements of urban warfare; or we look the other way, toward whatever the media are showing, and patiently wait for an unlikely war which would kindly allow us to remain exactly as we are, without any burden of change.

Fifty Years of Ethnic Conflict and Cohesion: 1945–1994

Noël Bonneuil, INED

This analysis examined ethnic conflict involving ethnic minorities and portrayed it in relation to political and socioeconomic factors.[4] It sought to address competing explanations for why ethnic conflict occurs.

The literature presents three basic theories of why ethnic conflict happens:

(1) instrumentalism: Following "rational choice" theory, this view considers ethnic violence as a means to attaining social, political, or economic goals.

(2) primordialism: This view stresses kinship, blood ties, or religious affiliation and views ethnic conflict as a consequence of group identity.

(3) constructivism: This view stresses the manufacture of ethnic identity and the crystallization of group identity for a particular societal purpose.

The study used the "Minorities at Risk" database, which contains information on conflict sequences involving 163 ethnic minority groups throughout the world between 1945 and 1994. The study built on prior work that sought to identify the underlying causes of these conflicts by comparing the living conditions of minorities to those of the dominant group, thereby producing a set of economic, political, and cultural indicators. The earlier work found that episodes of ethnic conflict were increasing and that the grievances of ethnic minorities were driven mainly by political and economic dynamics.

This study categorized the conflict episodes in the database as either nonviolent *protest*, which includes verbal opposition and demonstrations, or *rebellion*, which includes war and insurgency. The findings suggest that the roots of ethnic violence vary widely and that it is possible to find evidence to support both the instrumentalist and primordialist views.

Discrimination appears to be associated with protest if it is related to land and power; with war if it concerns social mobility; and with insurgency if it has to do with social customs. Migration from rural to urban areas and abroad is accompanied by a high degree of ethnic mobilization and rioting or war when social mobility is at stake.

The conclusions imply a relationship between conflict and lack of equitable social mobility, which suggests that conflict prevention policies need to pay more attention to promoting social mobility.

---

[4] This presentation is based on "Fifty Years of Ethnic Conflict and Cohesion: 1945–1994," *Journal of Peace Research*, vol. 37, no. 5, pp. 563–581, 2000.

APPENDIX

List of Participants

RAND

Julie DaVanzo

Brian Nichiporuk

David Adamson

Laurent Murawiec

RAND EUROPE

Stephan DeSpiegeleire

INSTITUT NATIONAL D'ÉTUDES
DÉMOGRAPHIQUES

Noël Bonneuil

Jean-Claude Chesnais

Philippe Bourcier de Carbon

SOCIÉTÉ DE STRATÉGIE

Eric de la Maisonneuve

ARMÉES

Général Jean-Loup Moreau, Bureau études et
stratégie militaire générale, Etat-Major des
Armées

Contre-Amiral Thierry d'Arbonneau, Etat-major
des Armées

Capitaine de Vaisseau Michel Pène, Direction du
Renseignement Militaire

Colonel Didier Tauzin, CEREMS, Centre des
Hautes études militaires

Prof. Gérard-François Dumont: Université
Paris-1

Gérard Chaliand, historien

Paul Fabra, économiste

Pierre Conessa, Ministère de la Défense

Yves Laloy, directeur de l'Institut des Relations
internationales

Selim El-Sayegh, directeur du DESS diplomatie
et relations internationales, Université de
Sceaux

Philippe Ratte, directeur de programme,
UNESCO